Friendly Giants:
California Gray Whales

by Sanjay Patel

PEARSON
Scott Foresman

Editorial Offices: Glenview, Illinois • Parsippany, New Jersey • New York, New York
Sales Offices: Needham, Massachusetts • Duluth, Georgia • Glenview, Illinois
Coppell, Texas • Sacramento, California • Mesa, Arizona

"The Friendlies"

Did you ever wonder what it feels like to touch a whale? Many people who visit Laguna San Ignacio know. That lagoon is located off the coast of Baja California, Mexico. California gray whales visit Laguna San Ignacio and other lagoons in the area every year. The whales migrate from the coast of Alaska to those warm lagoons to mate and have calves.

---

calves: baby whales

Laguna San Ignacio is the only place where whales come up to boats so that the people can touch them. The first time this happened was in 1976. It happened to a village fisherman named Francisco Mayoral, who was fishing in his boat. The whales always came close to his boat, but never right up to it. But one day it happened—one calf came up to the boat, and then its mother followed.

Soon other whales were coming up to the boats. The fishermen called them *las ballenas amistosas*, which means "the friendly whales" in Spanish. In English, these whales are now called "the friendlies."

People have many ideas about why "the friendlies" come up to boats. Some of these ideas are based on scientific study. Other ideas are based on people's feelings when they see or touch "the friendlies." While we don't know why the whales come up to the boats, we do know many other facts about the gray whale.

Facts

Population: There are about 26,000 California gray whales.

Size: The California gray whale is 35 to 50 feet long and weighs 40,000 to 80,000 pounds. Newborn calves are about 15 feet in length and weigh about 1,500 pounds.

Like all whales, the gray whale has a thick layer of blubber to keep it warm. This layer can be ten inches thick during feeding time. It gets thinner when the whales cut down on eating to migrate.

Feeding: Gray whales eat the tiny creatures that live near the bottom of the ocean. When they are feeding, they can eat a ton of food a day!

When gray whales feed, they suck sand into their mouths. Then, with their tongue, they push the sand out of the sides of their mouths and through the baleen. The creatures that were in the sand get trapped in the baleen. That is how the whales get their food.

---

blubber: fat

GRAY WHALE

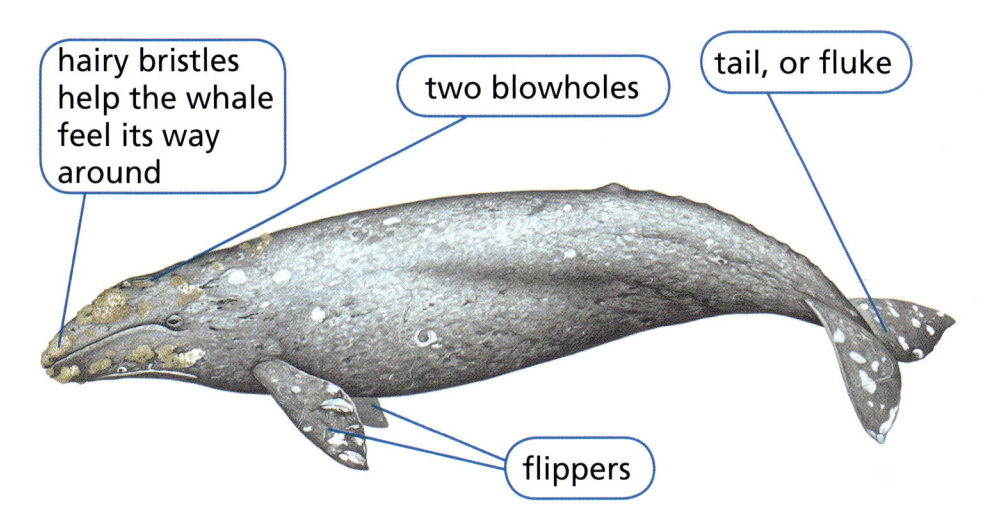

- hairy bristles help the whale feel its way around
- two blowholes
- tail, or fluke
- flippers

35–50 feet long

The gray whale has a long, narrow shape that helps it move through the water faster.

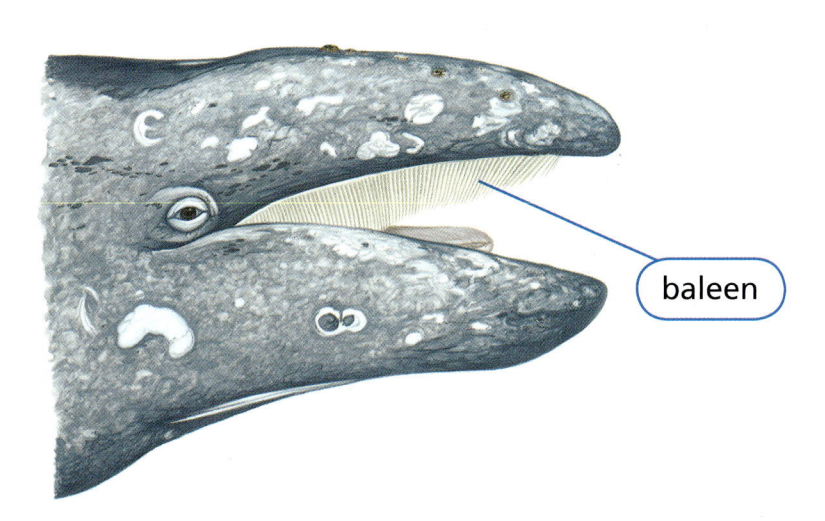

- baleen

Instead of teeth, the gray whale has plates of baleen which work like combs to filter the whale's food.

The salty water in the lagoons helps the calves float.

Calves: Female gray whales have one calf every two years. The calves nurse for seven months and can drink about 50 gallons of milk each day. This helps them build up the blubber they will need for the colder waters around Alaska.

The calves stay with their mothers in the lagoons for up to three months. The mothers teach them to swim against the currents in the lagoons. This is good practice for the calves, because they need to be able to swim in the strong currents of the open sea. They also need to be good swimmers in the ocean to get away from predators such as killer whales and sharks.

---

nurse: drink milk from their mother

Migration: California gray whales make one of the longest migrations of any mammal. The distance they travel can be up to 14,000 miles round trip. California gray whales spend the summer feeding in the arctic waters off Alaska. In the fall, when those waters begin to freeze over, the whales swim south to the warm lagoons off the west coast of Baja California. This journey takes two to three months, with most whales getting to the lagoons around January. They spend the winter there, finding mates and having their calves. Then, in early spring, when the calves are strong enough, the whales travel back to the cold northern waters.

Migration route of the California gray whale.

→ Major Whale Migration Routes
■ Summer Locations
■ Winter Locations

FACTS AND FEELINGS

The California gray whale is the only kind of whale that does not give birth in the open sea. Scientists wonder why the gray whales have their calves in the Baja California lagoons instead. They think it's because in the lagoons the water is warmer, saltier, and shallow. The salt in the water helps the calves float until they learn to swim. And predators can't swim in shallow water, so the calves are safe.

People who see "the friendlies" in Laguna San Ignacio like very much that such a massive animal comes near them. They like petting the whales, whose skin feels rubbery.

Now that you know more about the California gray whale, why do you think the whales come to the lagoons every winter?

---

shallow: not deep   **rubbery:** like rubber

Extend Language | Whale Migration Words

These words can be used to describe the migration of gray whales.

Adjectives	Nouns	Verbs
• long	• journey	• stay
• warm	• Pacific Ocean	• spend
• cold	• coast	• swim
	• distance	• migrate